LET'S MAKE A TENT

JACK STOKES

DAVID McKAY COMPANY, INC. ● NEW YORK

Copyright © 1979 by Jack Stokes • All rights reserved • ISBN: 0-679-20778-3 • LC: 79-2084
Printed in the United States of America. Cataloging in Publication Data can be found on p. 32.

How would you like to sleep overnight in a tent or
take it on a camping trip?

You can make your own tent—one that is just the right size for you and a friend to share.

The cloth for your tent can vary, depending on how you plan to use the tent.

If you just want a tent for your backyard and won't stay in it when it rains, almost any material will do. You can use old sheets, drapes, fabric shower curtains, or a patchwork of several different materials. You can also use plastic, but if your tent is closed up for the night, moisture may collect on the inside. By morning, you might feel a bit soggy.

For a tent that gives more protection from the weather and will be used on camping trips, you can buy muslin, poplin, twill, duck or nylon aspen cloth. There are many other kinds of 100% cotton fabrics that can be used. Canvas is also good, but it makes a heavy tent and it is expensive.

You can buy water repellents to treat cloth that is not guaranteed to shed water.

A good tent should be waterproof and as lightweight as possible.

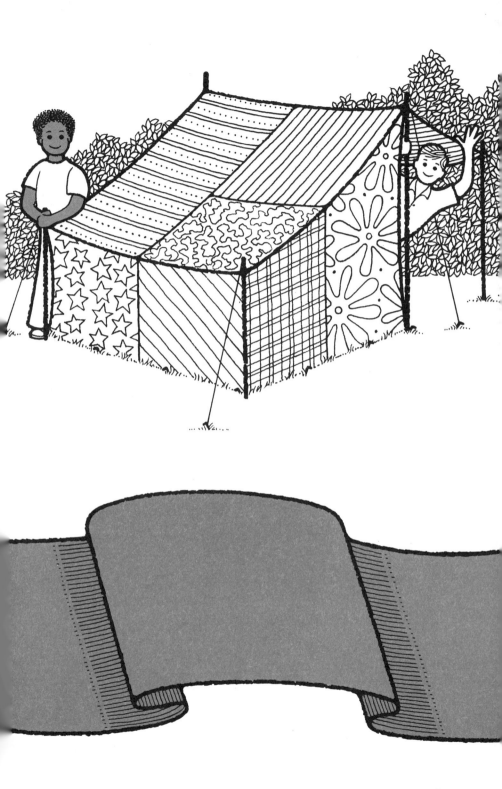

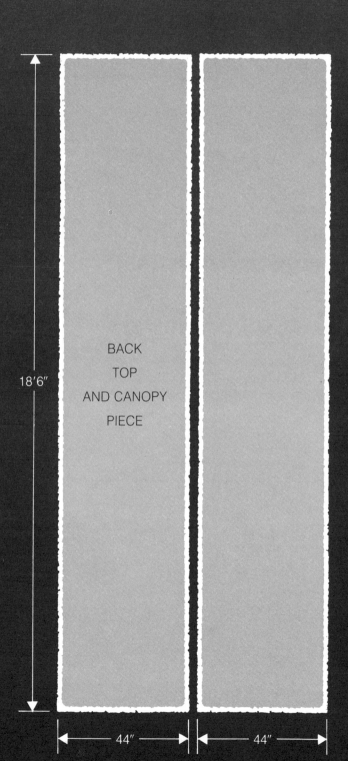

18'6"

BACK
TOP
AND CANOPY
PIECE

44" 44"

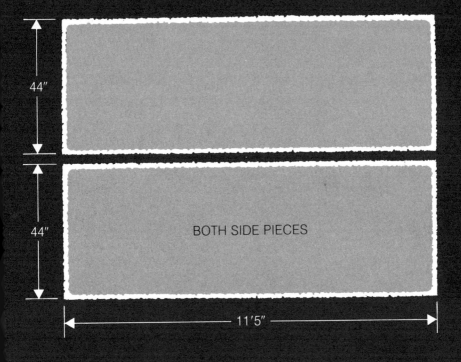

44"

44"

BOTH SIDE PIECES

11'5"

Here are diagrams showing the amount of material you need for a Baker tent. Because different kinds of material come in different widths, the number of yards you need may vary. You can scale the tent up or down a little in order to work easily with materials of different widths, or you can cut and piece the fabric to these dimensions.

The measurements in this book are for 44-inch-wide material. If you use the metric system, there is a conversion table on page 32.

You can make the back, roof, canopy-flap, and back sod cloth for your tent in one piece.

The sod cloth is a flap of the tent material, about 12 inches wide. It is turned under at the bottom of the back and sides to help keep out insects, wind, and small animals.

Cut two lengths of your 44-inch-wide material, each 18 feet, 6 inches long. Put the long edges together, side by side, and let them overlap 1½ inches. Use straight pins to hold the pieces in place. You can bind them together with a good waterproof glue made especially for awnings, sails, and tents. This will prevent water from seeping through the seams. Follow your product's instructions for a permanent, waterproof seam. Or, you can ask someone with a sewing machine to stitch the two pieces of material together. A flat-felled seam is the strongest seam for joining the material in your tent, but several other kinds of seams can also be used.

After the two long pieces of material are joined together, either glue or sew a 1-inch hem at both ends.

SOD			
CLOTH	BACK	ROOF	CANOPY FLAP

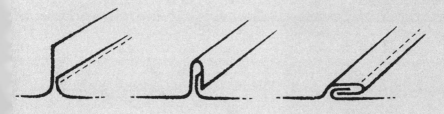

Now you can use this approximate 7-foot by 18-foot piece of material to make a lean-to. It will not give as much protection from the wind and rain as a tent. But it can be a temporary shelter in good weather.

Sew the middle of a 2-foot-long piece of twill tape, ¾ inches wide, to each of the four corners of the material. Measure 9 feet on both long edges of the material, and sew tapes at these two points. These six tapes are only for a lean-to, not for a tent.

Here are several ways to pitch your lean-to. You probably can think of even more.

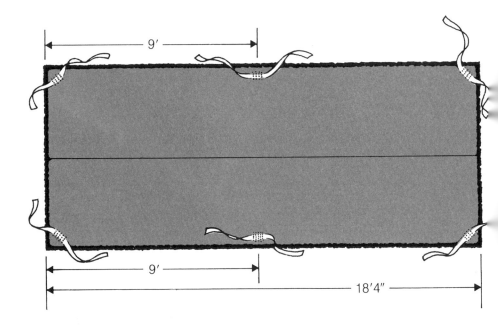

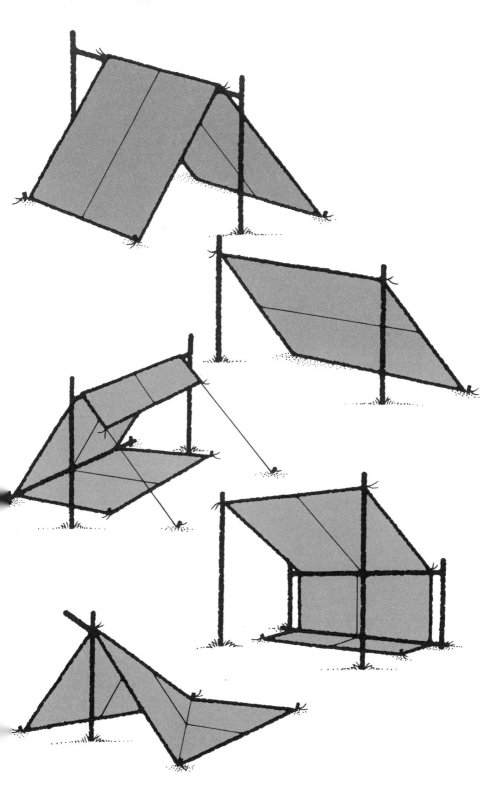

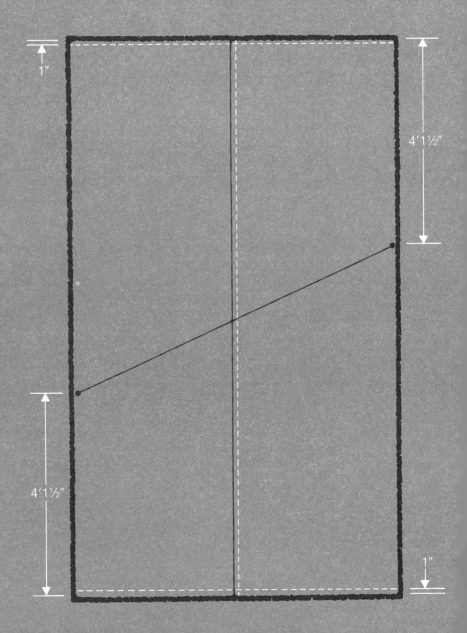

1"

4' 1 ½"

4' 1 ½"

1"

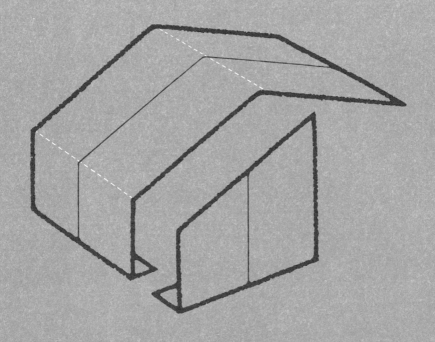

If you'd like to continue with a sturdier, weather-resistant and insect-proof tent, cut two more lengths of the 44-inch-wide fabric to 11 feet, 5 inches long.

Pin these two pieces side by side, on the long edge, with a 1½-inch overlap. Glue or sew them together, as you did with the back-roof piece. Also make a 1-inch hem at either end.

Now, holding the material vertical, make a mark 4 feet, 1½ inches up from the lower left-hand corner. From the upper right-hand corner, make a mark 4 feet, 1½ inches down on that edge. Connect these two marks with a diagonal line and cut the material on that line. This makes two large trapezoid shapes that will be the sides of your tent.

Measure from one end of the 18-foot piece of
material and put marks on both long edges at 1 foot
and at 4 feet. Place the back-roof piece so that each
long edge overlaps the short end of one tent side.
Line them up on the bottom edges. The 4-foot marks
on the back-roof piece should fall 1½ inches below
the top corner on the short edge of each tent side.
Pin the pieces together with a 1½-inch overlap.

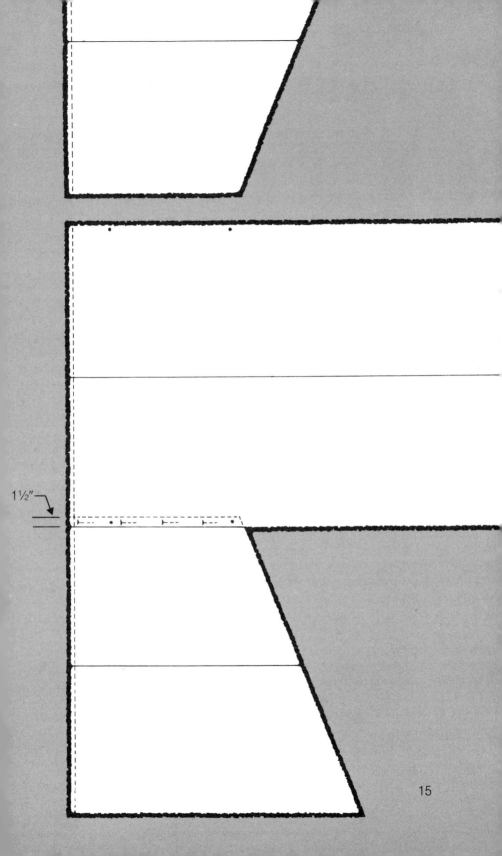

1½″

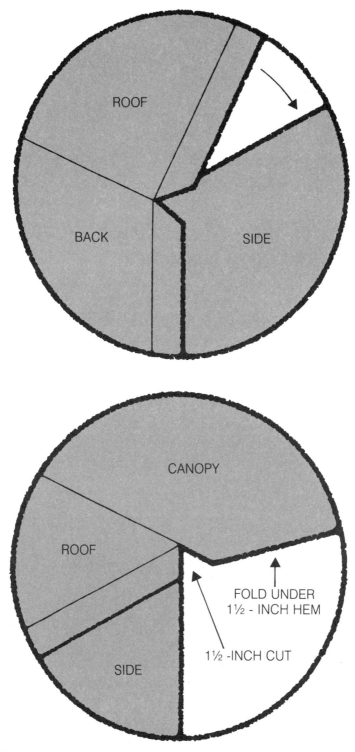

16

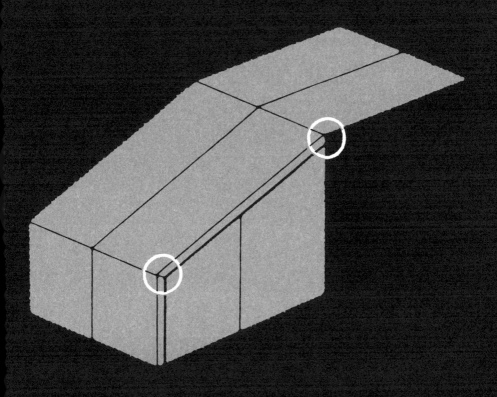

Cut V–shaped notches at the 4-foot marks on the
back-roof piece. Fold the fabric here and continue to
overlap and pin the sides of the back-roof piece 1½
inches over the top slanted edges of the tent sides.
When you reach the top front corners of the tent, snip
a 1½-inch cut on the edge of the back-roof piece.
Continue to fold the 1½ inches under the canopy
for a hem.

You can now glue or sew the back-roof piece to the
sides of your tent. Do not glue or sew the material
from the hem to the 1-foot marks. This will complete
the basic tent shape—a back, a slanting roof, a front
canopy-flap, and two sides.

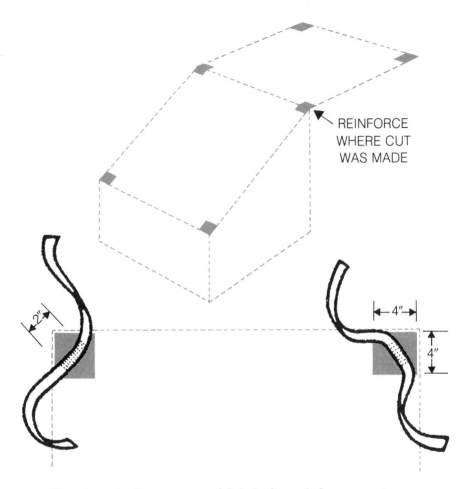

REINFORCE
WHERE CUT
WAS MADE

2"

4"

4"

Cut six 4-inch squares of fabric for reinforcements. Glue or sew one of the squares at each corner of the tent roof and the two outer corners of the canopy-flap. Make sure the squares at the front corners of the tent roof are attached so that they will keep the material from tearing where you made the 1½-inch cut to form the canopy.

To these six patches sew the middle two inches of 2-foot-long strips of ¾-inch twill tape. These should be sewn (not glued) very securely because they will receive the most stress when the tent is pitched.

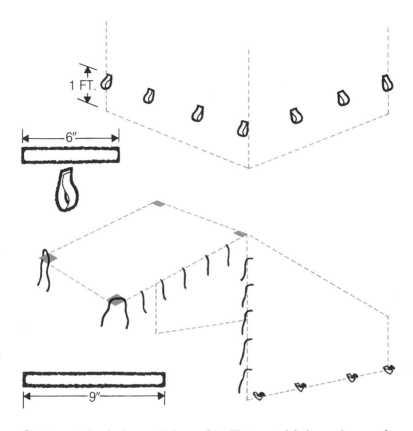

Cut ten 6-inch-long strips of twill tape. Make a loop of each strip and glue or sew one to each of the four bottom corners of the tent. Put a loop approximately every 28 inches across the bottom, on the back, and on both sides. Remember that the bottom edge of the tent is 1 foot in from the end of the material to allow for the sod cloth. These loops are for tent pegs.

To fasten the front flap down during high winds or rain, you will need twenty 9-inch ties. Cut the ties from your ¾-inch twill tape and glue or sew them securely every 12 inches along both front edges of the tent and both side edges of the canopy-flap. Use the tent ties at the corners of the canopy flap and tie them to the front tent peg loops for the bottom ties.

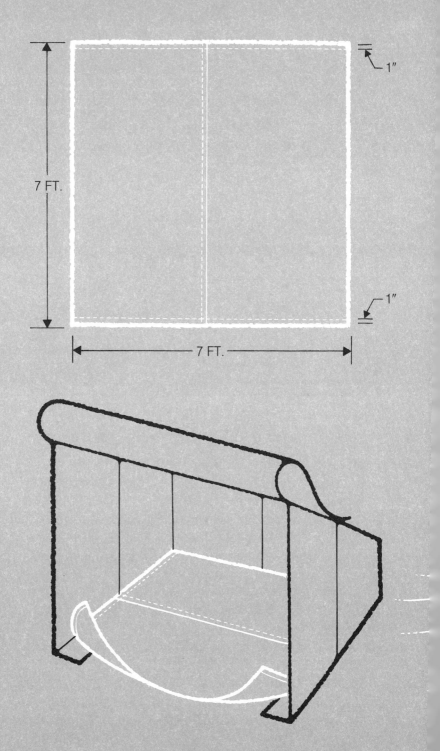

7 FT.

7 FT.

1"

1"

A tarp flooring in your tent will help protect you from dirt, moisture, and ground insects. You can make a tarp floor from heavy canvas, plastic, or any fabric that can withstand the wear and tear of shoes and edges of objects in your gear.

The flooring should be approximately 7 feet by 7 feet, the same size as the inside of your tent. You can sew two 7-foot lengths of 44-inch-wide material together, using a flat-felled seam for strength. Then sew or glue a 1-inch hem on the unfinished ends of the material.

The tarp floor is placed on the top of the back and side sod cloths.

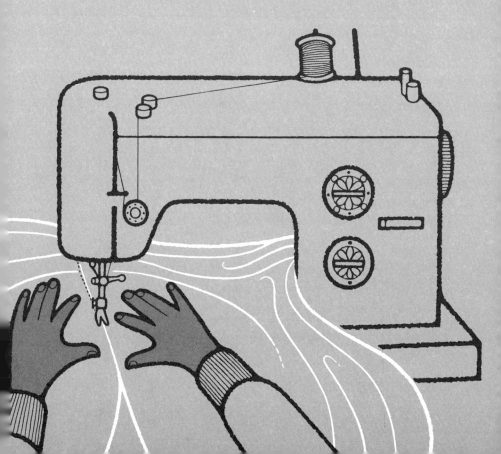

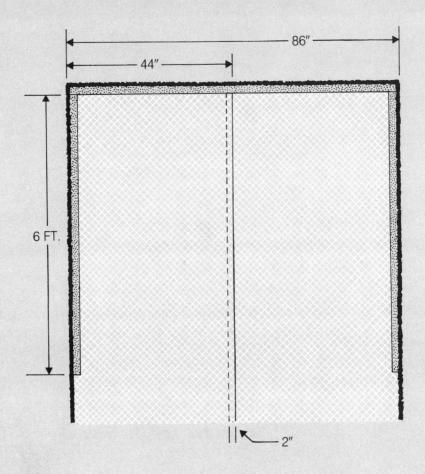

In good camping weather, you can leave the front flap of your tent up all night to get plenty of fresh air. But you will need a mosquito net over the open front end of your tent to keep out flying insect visitors.

Cut two 7-foot lengths of 44-inch-wide fabric suitable for a mosquito net, such as tulle, cheesecloth, or fine mesh. Place the pieces side by side, overlapping 2 inches, and glue or sew them together.

Using ¾-inch Velcro, glue or sew a strip across the

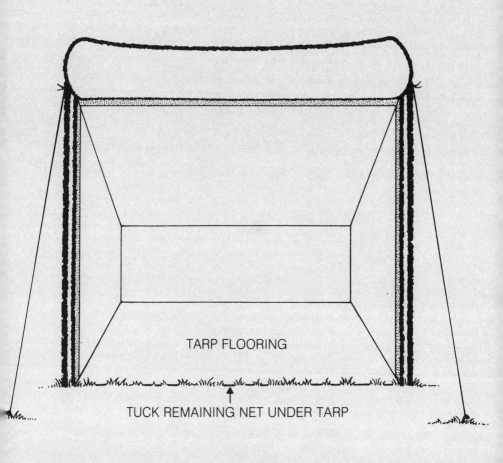

TARP FLOORING

TUCK REMAINING NET UNDER TARP

top of the netting. Then put 6-foot-long strips down the sides. Make sure that all the Velcro is on the same side of the netting, with the tooth side of the Velcro facing outward.

Sew or glue the corresponding strips of Velcro across the inside of the top front edge of the tent and down the inside of the front edges.

Now you can put up your insect barrier whenever you need it. There will be approximately a foot of material left at the bottom to tuck inside under the tarp flooring.

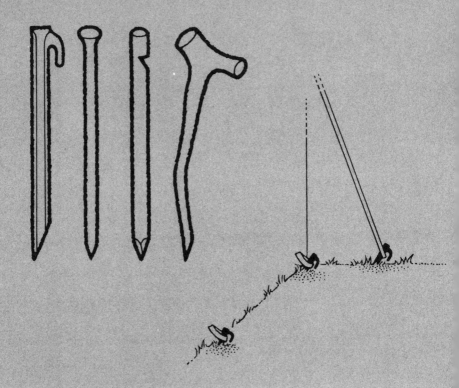

You will need sixteen tent pegs. Ten of these go through the 6-inch loops along the bottom of the tent to hold it down. The other six will be used to hold the guy ropes when you pitch your tent.

Tent pegs should be 9 to 12 inches long. You can buy tent pegs or long railroad spikes, or make pegs out of pieces of dowel or small forked branches of trees.

One end of each peg should be pointed so that you can drive it into the ground. The other end should be notched to keep the loops from slipping off.

The pegs are pounded into the ground at a 60° angle from the ground, with the points toward the tent and the tops pointing away from the tent.

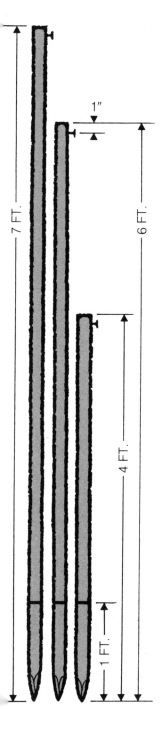

You can buy aluminum or wooden tent poles or you can make them yourself out of 1⅛-inch dowels. Aluminum is good because it is lightweight. However, in a thunderstorm, metal will attract lightning more than wood, so metal poles are not as safe as wooden ones.

You will need two 7-foot tent poles for the front of the tent; two 6-foot tent poles for the outer edge of the canopy; and two 4-foot poles for the back of your tent. Sharpen one end of each of the poles and put a heavy mark with ink 1 foot from the point on each pole. The mark will show you when you have driven the pole in the ground 1 foot—the right height for your tent.

Next, pound a 1-inch nail into each pole about an inch from the unpointed end. Leave approximately ⅜ of an inch sticking out from the pole. When you fasten the tent ties above the nails, they won't slide down the pole.

The canopy poles are a foot shorter than the front tent poles so the canopy will slope away from the tent.

Now you are ready to pitch your tent.

Find a high, open, level spot. If the ground slopes slightly, be sure the tent is placed so you can sleep with your head higher than your feet. Tents should face away from the wind and rain. Otherwise, try to face your tent to the east, as wind and rain are more likely to come from the west in most locations.

Make sure the area for your tent is clear of rocks, branches, roots, trash, and insect nests. The ground should be dry, with good drainage away from the tent, and not in the path of water run-offs. Don't pitch a tent under old trees with dead branches that might fall on it.

Lay your tent on its side to pitch it. Pound tent pegs through the four side loops and into the ground. Then drive the front and back tent poles into the ground at the corners. Make sure the nails at the top face away from the tent. Raise and tie that side of the tent securely above the nails. Next, peg down the back of the tent and drive the other back tent pole at that corner. Tie the tent to it and peg down the remaining side. Now you can drive the other front pole, and tie the tent to that.

You can use clothesline or heavy wrapping twine to run guy ropes from the four poles at the corners of the tent. Tie them over the tent ties on the poles.

Then stretch the ropes out diagonally, about 3 feet from the tent, and fasten them to tent pegs. Use a taut line hitch so you can easily change the tension on the lines.

Drive in the poles for the canopy-flap and tie it to them. Wrap the ties both above and below the nails so the canopy won't slip down or blow off. Attach guy ropes, the same way as before.

Tents should be stretched fairly smooth so that water will drain off. However, water temporarily shrinks

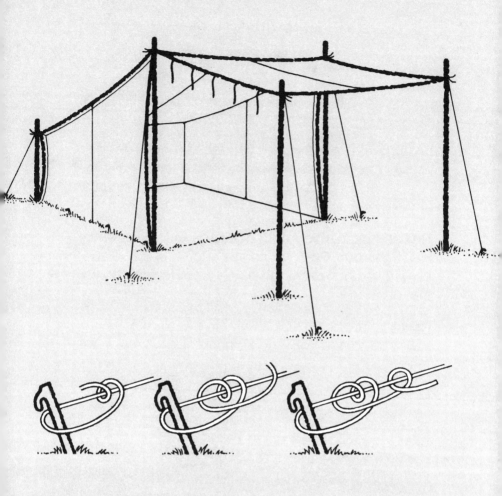

cotton so the ties and ropes must have enough play to prevent the material from being stretched so tight that it rips. Loosen the guy lines, if necessary, when it rains. Avoid touching the inside of your tent when it is raining, because the water will drip through the material wherever you touch it.

Smooth out the sod cloth inside the tent and lay the tarp flooring.

You can attach the mosquito net to the top and then the sides of the tent whenever you need it.

If your tent is damp when you take it down, dry it out as soon as you get home. Packing a tent away when it is damp will cause mildew and rot. Shake or brush any dirt off your tent, too.

Roll and bundle your tent neatly so that loose ends won't get torn. Pegs and poles should be bundled separately to prevent the points from making holes in the fabric.

Now you are ready to go camping again whenever you want to and you'll be able to enjoy your tent for many years.

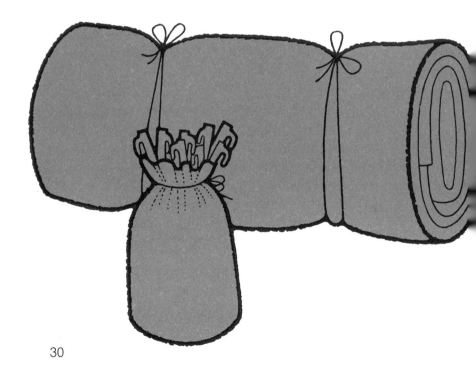

31

If you use the metric system follow these substitute (not equivalent) measurements to make your tent:

⅜ inch. . . . . . . 1.0 cm

¾ inch. . . . . . . 1.9 cm

1 inch. . . . . . . 2.5 cm

1⅛ inch. . . . . . . 2.9 cm

1½ inch. . . . . . . 3.8 cm

2 inches. . . . . . . 5.1 cm

4 inches. . . . . . . 10.2 cm

6 inches. . . . . . . 15.2 cm

9 inches. . . . . . . 22.9 cm

1 foot. . . . . . . 30.5 cm

2 feet. . . . . . . 61.0 cm

28 inches. . . . . . . 71.1 cm

3 feet. . . . . . . 91.5 cm

44 inches. . . . . . . 1.12 meters

4 feet. . . . . . . 1.22 meters

4 feet 1½ inches. . . . . . . 1.26 meters

6 feet. . . . . . . 1.83 meters

7 feet. . . . . . . 2.13 meters

9 feet. . . . . . . 2.74 meters

11 feet 5 inches. . . . . . . 3.48 meters

18 feet 6 inches. . . . . . . 5.64 meters

Library of Congress Cataloging in Publication Data

Stokes, Jack.
  Let's make a tent.

  SUMMARY: Presents instructions for making a tent, including what fabric to use, how to make measurements, and how to combine the parts.
  1. Tents—Juvenile literature. [1. Tents. 2. Handicraft] I. Title.
TS1860.S76   685'.53   79-2084
ISBN 0-679-20778-3